Mirrors Doors and
High Towers

Mirrors Doors and High Towers

Selected poetry

By

Ulrike Lüdicke

Bibliografische Information der Deutschen Nationalbibliothek
Die Deutsche Nationalbibliothek verzeichnet diese Publikation in der
Deutschen Nationalbibliografie; detaillierte bibliografische Daten sind
im Internet über http://dnb.d-nb.de abrufbar

Umschlaggestaltung: Stephanie Rosenau

Umschlagabbildung: Ulrike Lüdicke

Herstellung und Verlag: Books on Demand GmbH,
Norderstedt

ISBN-13: 978-3-8370-5542-9

Contents

2002

2003

2004

2005

2006

2007

2008

This poem was actually done for an assignment I got in my English as a second language class in the US. Even though I wrote it in 2000 it's still mostly me, so...

Unsteady walking through the whole life
Like a bird that cannot fly.
Right behind the next edge looking
Into the face of a stranger. Thinking "You
Know him. I guess."
Endless wandering through nowhere.

Lifetime is struggling
Ump-teen times fighting against
Everybody. Hoping all the time not to
Delay anything more. Never
In peace with herself.
Cold is everywhere,
Kindness very rare to find. Trying to
Enjoy every single second.

2002

Countless the days of unawareness
Troubling those who deem to see
Further than others would guess
Yet there's just one goal: dignity

Forever is ever gone with the wind
Hope has left faithful creatures
Blown asunder without any hint
Unclear now are all features

In whatever hope has stayed
I built up and none too late
Foundations of a future still to come

So pain will leave and lone is he
Who starts to feel so close to thee
That past and present, future yet will see it done

~~~

Fading into shadows
As though never have been
There is nothing that grows
The world is just mean

So when things do change
They go out of range
Passing into the grey
And nothing will stay

~~~

Her eyes, I saw them
Going straight past me
All of a sudden
Pure darkness came on
Fear struck me
Just wanted to leave
Greatest desire of safety and home
Then it was gone
All forebodings faded
Wisdom grounded
Will always go on
Do what is said
None to regret
And they were lost
Those eyes that I saw
The wish then came up
Desire to know
What were they hiding?
Where did they go?

~~~

Long ago when time was young
I did not care what's right what's wrong
So now the present overwhelms
That old is new and without realms
A country boundless borderless
Is doomed to nothing more than caress
By one as big and proud to think
Wherever right wherever wrong may sink
My fate is bound to that of yours
And never will it choose another course

~~~

Nothing can prevent
What is to come
Ere long it was planned
None knows where from
So it may be
Unchanged in this world
Those blinded will see
Yet no word is heard

~~~

When will life reveal purpose
When will people change minds
Those deriving from darkness
Never kept hidden never arrayed
In order to change what they have done
Nothing will differ from old ways for long

~~~

2003

A mirror reflecting my very soul
Showed my dreams and where they go
For all my life is but a dream
Like driving rollercoaster on a stream

And wonders oh so great
That happen all day long
But soon now will they fade
Remaining memory is strong

In wishing hopes then only stay
Tasks that one day they won't sway
Then all the wonders also might remain

And this time the mind is not
The place where only god
Could marvel at these human thoughts

~~~

Ancient was I when they came
Waiting for them when they came
Desperate was I when they came
Devastated about their arrival

Knowing what fate had planned
Knowing what had to happen
Knowing what would kill too many
And that without there wouldn't be any life

Do I have a choice?
I certainly have the power
Do I have the right to change
Consequences definitely are too great

~~~

Another thought invading minds
As brutal as it always finds
The way that people handle things
And matters, pulling strings
Rather harsh are methods
Of dealing with problems facing wrath
Somehow miraculously escaping death
Inferior is darkest night
And none can find a single light

~~~

Are we rightfully claiming everything our own
The world is filled with great wonders
Yet all of them have grown alone
We deem our work greater than god's

There is nothing that stops such ideas
It is the lonely that fears
Consequences of actions to be taken
And if I'm not absolutely mistaken
That would mean the end of all

~~~

Cruel are those ignoring time
Just unaware of their own crime
Can't they show some dignity
Ridiculous behavior leaving doubt
In yourself amongst that crowd
So hope that further you might see
Has left and melting into grey
A part of the crowd you are to stay

~~~

Deep in thoughts
Always awake
Restrained by wonders
Fighting for your sake

Expecting defeat
Always defensive
Keeping some hope
Although it seems lost

Is it not foolish
Keeping all faith
Ever within you
To never fade

All is ever aware
That end is to all
So why then dare
The deepest of falls

My world is grey
This never will change
For my heart is cold
And yearning for leave

Even though not understanding
What you're fighting for
I do grant you respect -
Without me in the lore

The end then could be
That my self is fading
While you with your hope
Could keep this world here

~~~

Don't anger me in my possession
Of what will always be my own
How easy is to raise aggression
Among these people that just frown
The other by their deepest core
As if life created only one will
Neglecting all to live up for
And surely they'll go on until:
Maybe they find another goal

~~~

Encouraging is the thought of
Little hobbitses finding rings of power
In dark mines facing evil creatures.
Just such ongoings
Allow those deeming themselves
Hopeless the dare to dream.

Joking, jumping, bouncing of the walls surely not
Overestimating things too tall
Rings are fancy must be
Don't say anything else can't be
Attitudes? What's that?
Nothing can shock. Is that a lack?

Whenever time comes
On goes the road high above far
Over all there is
Down to the earth that is to kiss

~~~

Goodness Lord
I seek thy word
Thy counsel
Hear!
My pleading
Please!
Can't be that ere
My life upon this -
This world has ended

Before I have taken my leave
I seek thy word
I seek to leave
And leave behind
A part of mine

~~~

Grim thought
Dark room
Cold walls
Nothing in bloom
Fear crosses the mind
One seeks to go

~~~

Huge doors with fear laid upon
Frightening to those putting their eyes there on
Clueless of what they might hide
Yet one is fully aware of their pride

Staggering shuddering fainting nobody dares
A long look upon them for it not spares
Any of them - none to redeem
Ageless still stone-aged they seem
Forgotten they'll ever remain
Some do remember and live in pain

~~~

Impossible has been the night
Arraying pieces in new light
Replacing some by others
Others even more from deepest core
Get crushed so utterly
That sense is lost none knows what for

~~~

In lasting thoughts is kept awake
The things that always are at stake
Innumerable detesting minds
Aligning those of different kinds

Measure a treasure not on your own
Ending up you might, utterly alone
And left are those, maybe, that care
Hope! They take the treasure and share

Beneath mankind's spirits at last
Lies hidden a huge mound growing fast
Darkness inside uncounted for
Nowhere to find an entering door

~~~

Incredible when inside out
Is turned the cheering crowd
Amazing is when gazing through the rows
Their eyes in which the fear just grows
Expecting hoping for the worst to happen now
But the question coming is: And how?
Yet rather should it be a stronger Why

For they are cheering some will cry
Surprisingly or better not they do not care
There really is no punishment you spare
Events shall never take this course another time
Cause they could then be doing crime

~~~

Is it true or just fake
Ought one only take
The needed goods
For one alone and not to share
With others where
Else could one then find this care
Selfish people over there
Just too happy would they be
If you do start with dignity

~~~

It came suddenly into my thoughts
That life is what ought to be
A good joke like or even a simple game
Gambling for existence
Fighting for nothing
And loosing just everything they own
A lot there is but only the crown
Breaks rules and creates their own
Destruction that brings for all in the tomb

~~~

It is as said a mighty task
Fulfilled in dreams and only there
Though really hard to tell from where
So don't stop thinking go and ask

Even if people do wonder rather fast
That thoughts and skills forevermore
Are following an elder lore
And open is one world at last

The pictures flowing through such mind
Are of oldest, purest, greatest kind

~~~

It was the night before Christmas
Then I saw what used to be a dream
So uttermost empty did it seem
It filled itself - surprising eh?
No seriously I should not stay
With minor details of some holy night
Sure the moon was shining bright
And stars were all around blinking side by side
Snow had fallen so my garden all in white
Invited me to stroll a bit
I though was not at all that fit
For my plan had been an early slumber
In order to awake then soon
Finding henceforth a great number
Of presents yay what fun
I'm trailing of again damn me what shame
Now where was I?

Yes this walk I took through holy night
Too much light just too bright
But anyway what else to say - Right!
So did I walk not wander far
When faint another light appeared
A strange one certainly
Now what could that be?
My grammy often told
Stories from a book too old
Forgot its name again what shame
Well surely looked suspicious
New light not that bright more evil?
Stupid me!
Went closer of course
And did I see?
Oh yes I saw
What do you think
Holy spirit, angels even more
Nah I wish
Some nasty kids had had some fun
On me how should it then be
Put on fire my precious only one
My Christmas Tree

~~~

Lands once owned by my people
Shall never reveal their secrets
To anyone that is not family
Death awaits daring impostors
True wisdom of ancient times
To those that deserve them
For long ago we gave ourselves

In order to rescue their lives
They don't remember never will
So we are doomed to live with them
Hidden among those unknown
Always threatened to vanish for good

~~~

No doubt there is of things to come
Another day unaware where from
In time the understanding of your mind
Blows endless thoughts for them to find
The truth which tries a hiding place in all
For hiding things that are this tall
Is a complicated task indeed
And even if you are of creed
Much nobler than the others are
Your sight should still not wander far

~~~

No more scolding me please
I have been trying to achieve
What you asked for now I beg
Admit my self not where I lack

All those keeping their distance
To their surrounding and fence
Themselves just in order to
Avoid some personal waterloo
Cannot expect of me the same
So I'm not the only one to blame

~~~

Numbers confusing mind
Head whirling as if blind
Winds blowing through emptiness
Light that is better to caress
Orders to follow
Some rather hollow
In the end there's hope
Understanding in order to cope
With filling thought
That had been brought

~~~

Once lost in darkness
Once lost in nowhere
You hardly ever find
You way out of hell

So rare is kindness
And life just not fair
Let's you feel blind
Who cares oh well

~~~

Riddles of human nature
Strange to all of us
Weird and helpless
No power over anything
Steadiness unknown
Kindness too rare often just fake
Open minds get crushed

Hopes fade
Emptiness remains
Life stains
And lone fights he not adjusting

~~~

Somewhere in a hidden land
I can see what's real
Can touch it by hand
My dreams are there
Meaning a great deal
But after all I can not feel
Then real or surreal

So I live life
Mine, my own as good as I can
And everywhere I go
Seeing people distinguishing their thoughts
What's what ought to be brought
As surreal into the minds
Of those not caring about
The difference of both

I cannot tell
Whether difference exists
Some say once dreams come to pass somewhere
In a hidden land where they're called realists

~~~

Start a life!
Just go on forward
Don't look back
Never dare taking a step
To where you've been before
Just go on
Put your eyes on new worlds
Explore and learn
Do not return
Just go on
And you will see
Life will never ever be
So peaceful, calm and wonderful
As you remember it had been

~~~

Surprise!
You're dead
Finally someone gotcha
Too bad
Really sad

Cry!
For the dead
He had been your friend
Still bad
And really sad

Joy!
He is dead
To all that despised
Not bad

Not really sad

Surprising is his departure
Makes some cry for him
Others will enjoy the future
Who actually cares what is bad
Enjoying life even though it's sad

~~~

The likelihood this undertakement may
Eventually find some sense by being
Apparently soo… unimportant
Might really prove rather difficult
So allowing them a certain freedom
Some dignity and pride alongside
Should grant more chances to ever be

~~~

Thus feeling the offence that intense
Ought to explain the internal urge
That one is seeking revenge to some degree
And though rational behaviour has ever been
A thing of most strange fantasy to all
We should start somewhere showing
What we call humanity
Thus gaining a new strength since unknown

~~~

Whenever feeling hardship drawing closer
Retreat is what the answer is
Whenever pain and fear get grosser
The answer given is return the same

That's mankind ever loathing one another
No change will be if come what may
The end is hate towards your dearest brother
No place you safely grow or even stay

~~~

Who are you to claim something that precious
Does life not teach people of your kind
To hide in holes where none can find
You and your kindred
Never leave those places
Did mommy not say so
It is not safe out there
And really that's the way things go
Hide and never reveal yourselves
A threat you are
To you and this world
Leave it and peace might return

~~~

Winged creatures seen only at night
Glowing eyes detesting the light
Stronger than any known force

Feared by mankind for ages already
Blamed for actions only Lucifer would do
In the end there's no place to go to

Resistance grows hidden among the unknown
Steady always and always on
Some day they surely will rise

So what will then be?
Do these creatures know dignity?
What are they like what will we see?

Are we to change to the better
Then greeting those ancient friends
Open and true in peace forevermore

Uncertain, unlikely still all the same
We always need someone to blame
Past is gone and will never return

~~~

2004

And as they came into the light
All darkness thus fell from them of
As if the sun shone ever bright
And all will last in happiness and love

But that is just a dream too great
Beyond a glimpse of true reality
Busted is that present state
Bragging always further you can see

Count on nothing to be true
Call others to be aiding you
Cast spells on castles raised alone

Do never leave your realm unguarded
Dare not to let them get started
Deep down is light - a single dome

~~~

Arrogance they call a fatal flaw
Insolence is always present with
Hardship proves a life so raw
True feelings then turn rather stiff

Nothing's done about this though
They live on ignorant forevermore
Their heads they will just never bow
Nor will they see what all is for

~~~

Bright new day warm and gay
Says just what people always want
Cold and wet and dark and grey
Is pure dislike yet not to grant
Their wishes fully and complete
Brings anger hatred such emotion
As if you keep the royal seat
Totally responsible for every notion

~~~

Come all ye faithful creatures
Walk with me along my way
My bright and glowing feature
Will bring you through the day
Save and sound and all around
Never will you find then harm
To this promise I'll be bound
So you have a home, dry and warm
I expect respect fully from you all
My temper can be really bad

So praise me put up temples tall
Or else my mood will fall - so sad
You pity little children human kind
Seek leadership in your own mind

~~~

Come on why do you bother
Why do you care
How come you falter
Nobody can alter the past
It's there and will last
Fall all eternity and ever on
But you can see it might grasp it
Then hold it tight and keep it
And thereby live through it

~~~

Dark have ancient times been
Would never want to live there
Creepy muddy brutal state
Making life hell and unfair
But had it really been like that
So horrible unaccounted for
Imagine time in thousand years
Would they like being here today
The present seems to be so great
That nothing else does matter more
Respect, knowledge should not fade
To somewhen be an ancient lore

~~~

Dark walls hardly to be made out
Gloomy light is there all about
Icy floor with decorated spring
Doors so countless seem to sing
A song of horror immortality
Grief and pain invisibility

~~~

Death they call me
End of everything
Yes the end came
Long ago so long
But still some staid
A messenger I'd been
Bringing news to allies
A moment so small
A thought that lingered
And all in a sudden
Death struck hard
When then I returned
All was gone for good

~~~

Devastating boring endless snoring
Senseless sticking to some fact
Arguing discussing bruised thoughts
Theorizing always on and beyond
Doing absolutely nothing of course
Ignoring the most simple things
And in the end time has been spent
To find no goal and that is all

~~~

Mirrors doors and high towers
Power sight and horror
Great deeds and gifts will turn
So then all good will burn

Blood will flow as from springs
Fear through all that survives
Hope faded already at the start
The upcoming time will be hard

They spared only the weakest
Created a mass easily controlled
A long time is yet to be passing by
Until a people might cease to cry

~~~

Reflections of so many things
The past gone by
What just now is
What might one day come true
A gate it is believed to be
Named after Phoenix from the ashes
A mirror, doorway through all times
Telling fate and destiny
That will be upon those standing before
Daring the judgment of the elders

~~~

Since I can remember thinking
My head is whirling blurry sight
All in all it feels like sinking
Deep into the darkest night

Desire keeping hope alive within
That one day we will be the same
With an ability to always fighting
And finding also some to blame

Whatever's going through this world
Unknown and not yet been of heard
Keeps up a sparkle of resistance

For what is there what we do know
Will always stay will always grow
To maybe then keep up existence

~~~

Sit down and think
            Now hard
You have to find some thought
            Won't come darn
Beloved merciful you think your thought
            Still won't come bugger
So what we do and what we think
To be controlled is hard a thing

~~~

Stains brown grey blame
Mainly not to gain anything
Vain all so much rain
And pain all the more
Greater and beyond
What we know
What we are for

Help leave stay retrieve my soul
Harsh world stormy stony ways
Raging wars and so much pain
Leave you just weak alone
And when at last world breaks
Destroyed is all that's ever been
A thought in stars might be a light
New chance new life without stains

~~~

That's my life my dream my goal
My world in which I state the rules
Intruders will find themselves soon broken
And I as lonely power will forever stay
These borders I set up too long ago
Will never fall nor crumble just a little bit
The reinforcements ever came and grew
That appearing cracks weren't only filled
But seemingly a whole new wall was built

~~~

Then see it coming watch it leaving
Bouncing circles round and round
Lost is gone there's no retrieving
Old things fade and only some reborn
That's how it goes without believing
Like all the endless waters, oceans wide
We might be hiding fearful not receiving
Not having granted wishes, deep delights

~~~

There you are arrived finally
Welcome in your new home
You are just as we expected
Perfect for this blue room

Nights will now be quite long
You are the heck of some work
But please don't get me wrong
We love you forever and on

How you grew over the years
Watching you roll on the floor
Always enjoying new things
That ever pass through our door

It's funny watching you play
With guns and toy soldiers
With your friends hide and seek
All through the neighborhood

Your first day of school ever
Everything's so neat and cool

Now you're smiling - not forever
Will you one day be the fool

I dearly hope you will grow up
Having all your wishes granted
Maybe on your desk a laptop
Lovely girlfriends all enchanted

Proud I am on days like these
Finished school on top of class
Survived the action years with all
This fun sport raising parental fears

A grandson we call our own
Almost jealous of your luck
And as the father is the son
You know Shakespeare's Puck?!

My parents now left long ago
My children are grown-up
I now am spending life alone
Since Mary's heart attack

A few last years I do have left
My life had not been bad
It started good just getting better
And somehow ended sad

~~~

What if I grow angry beyond what is good
What if life grows weary more than I should
What if all I desire just catches fire
And within my crumbling little world
I come to see this huge jerk

~~~

Whizzy, whirly, turning
Blurry, blinded, sparkles
Fading, fainting
Fighting, loosing, trying
Boosting, again loosing
Working hard, important
Thinking, sinking and yet
Again loosing
Then why again trying?
Have to!
So back to misty, foggy
Unclear dots of understanding

~~~

World falls crumbles fades
Keep walking
People dead blood yelling
Keep walking
Pain injuries diseases spread
Keep walking
Devastation brutal action that
Turns all evil out of men
Will follow ignorant aggression
Because they always kept on walking

2005

A breeze goes through the ocean
And all does freeze
A whirlwind blows within this silent motion
They've lost their ease
The walls that kept is all at bay
Are tiny now, so small so simple
When built they were so tall so great
How could that splendour dwindle

~~~

A kingdom in heaven to last eternally
Keeps all secrets formerly owned by mankind
And all its derivation
Guarding the past
Ensuring the future
Keeping up with its vast responsibility
That one day today's youngsters all grown up
Would reclaim their heirlooms and grow beyond

~~~

All throughout the darkest night
With uncertain fate and little delight
He struggled to finally do it all right
Set straight the old dept unpaid
Freeing both body and mind

~~~

Am tired am bored
Curiosity just lured
Me into fatigue
Made me fall asleep

~~~

Between inside beside intervened
And yet so it still seemed
All right and perfectly fine
Argh! Poor fools we are – all the time
When curiosity gets the better
When caution subsides
         Is lulled in with promise
When fate seems to strife
         Among our midst with emperors grace
All our dreams and hopes
Staring right at ones face
In such moment of great weakness
It then is that we poor fools
Receive a hard kick in our behinds

~~~

Business of heart and faith
Immortality and death
Life and all that is left
So many thoughts so many riddles
          never to be solved
The essence of what we are
          put into words abstract – out of grasp
So strange that we can define every thing
          except who we are

~~~

Dare not speak not think your thoughts
Dare not believe that you are you
Forever in control by others
Always them and never you
It matters not how wrong you are
Just wrath and egoistic thoughts
And anger is there oh so much
It grows on you and even fought
With all your might
The end then is you've left from sight

~~~

Do and don't
Should and just won't
Didn't and still doomed
Played everything by the books
No mistakes
Not even at a deeper look
Everything perfect and still
It just won't

Won't seem or look certainly not feel right
And those perfect mishappenings
Will keep you up at night

~~~

Drowning somewhere over there
When all's invisible – like dying breath
And though crying out for help
Should get attention from all over
Just silence answers
The water's grown so high above your head
The urge to live fades slowly with your life

~~~

Dull lethargic emptiness
Growing on me evermore
I Grieve myself and all there is
Just never can be found
Though searching always
Chances shrink just faster
As though never having been

~~~

Endearing beautiful gifted dutifully
Serving fate as though unwavering trust
Might strengthen existence
As though pretending to be blind
Without own thought would
Be your purpose in life

~~~

Even when entire worlds collapse
And darkness is there – all about
This lonely artefact will hold
And stand upright throughout – eternity

And when a sparkle of light returns to be
That messenger of a new rising lets the old myths
And hidden future emerge from that doorway
To greet those newcomers that would too soon be
Just a faint memory in that mirror of time
Like all the others

~~~

Grand schemes work always better
Than just that simple thought of yours
You cannot see or judge the weather
That's passing now through this parcour
And when decisions then are made
Of reasoning for greater good
Take counsel not just from the great
Consider also common likelihood

~~~

Growth strength both at length
Nowhere near to ever disappear
And though everything goes evermore the same way
Sometimes when one stays and looks behind
Power and greatness he finds are to never be again
And then going on leaving the way
To choose a different array
A different growth

~~~

Guilt blame responsibilities priorities consequences
In the end a choice – demonic as can be
Life or living – to be or not to be
Does today outweigh everything else – just to be
What is nothingness like – what might have been

~~~

I am daughter of the sun and the night
A lonely creature torn between darkness and light
Firstborn Ancient and elder just as well as
A childish fool out to war against the verse

I am daughter of kings and queens emperors czars
Daughter of gods that once upon a time were
Last in a lineage so great and proud
Were they remembered all heads would be bowed

I am daughter of the past prophesied to rule the future
The light of two stars would give birth to a newborn
Brighter than anything that's ever been

~~~

In this almighty falsehood that came
Upon him whence all else fails and
Entire heights and lows loom shadowy
Over glowing mountains of doom though
Surely with purpose and all kinds of
Likelihoods the urges too come up t
Your fears stand up to what you should
Dare not face a moment close

~~~

It might not be seen
It might not be heard
Not felt not there at all
Yet still that faith and believe
Put into this thought
Make it so real
That everything and all
Reveres it adheres it fears it

~~~

Mastering all your given powers
Using them in a manner that could eventually
Even profit others than just yourself
And just when you dare not hope beyond hope
Dare not dream beyond what can be
          Grow stronger even – Lost thought
Goes wandering somewhere through empty minds
Meeting some thoughts some single some benign
Some boring most of them lame
And then it does some math and before it explores
There comes Amico adesse est
Pondering what that might mean
New thought new world beyond stars
New dream one's self without scars
And yet again some math

~~~

Mighty warships sail through seas of dawning emptiness
That's ever dull
With always same sight same sweet caress
And never ever full
And whence their captains call them out
        To fight an enemy beyond
Those fellas grumpy, stout and blond
        Will rise to only fall into the void

                        ~~~

Miracles happen never seen
Alone and hidden as though
        not having been ever at all
Often though tall just tiny and small
We keep looking for them always
Not finding where they affect us most

                        ~~~

Mystic dreams of ancient times rise
Seldom from those tightly locked doors
Yet on rare occasions – when they do
Make their way into a conscious mind
Those forgotten truths are awed at
And then to find them once again
Stored behind an open door

                        ~~~

Nightmares scare you minds than bother what to do
  And all in all there are not nearly as few
  Matters important – explanations then due
  Come not and they will argue
  Doubtless without success
  Over new possibilities

~~~

Sacred and holy visions
When unbound those truly ancient powers
We had and knew so long ago
Are unleashed and turn into a fire
Elder creatures might arise
And overwhelmed by wisdom and insight
Man does tend to utterly faint

~~~

The uttermost depths of my heart
Where all secrets are kept on guard
Harbour all hopes and dreams also
And whilst dwelling somewhere meaningful
Pretending nothing in your life's ever dull
Everything around just seems to grow

~~~

Though high and proud – all broken
That all so illustrious crowd – just woken
The shock went deep – through every bone
Dark creatures creep – to anyone alone
All protection they'd had – crumbled and faded

Now strangers they'd met – they're all hated
In raising a new wall – so very much higher
To stop the downfall – completing a vicious circle of fire

~~~

Thoughtfulness is some responsibility
It may seem gentle, nice, polite
But then since man is selfish first
And others then when own needs dulled
When dreams are dimmed may maybe
Enter into consciousness alas
Would it not rather be guilt than any true thought

~~~

Tired empty thought
Lost gone only when drought
Can be fought 'gainst
That ghastly enemy residing
In the depths of your soul
No matter how hard everyone's trying
Regardless of price or prize
These battles entire wars
Just destroy you utterly

~~~

Uncertain future and forgotten past
Make sure everything present won't last
Sincere regret yet wrong path
Lead to a fatal blast
And then daring just one more step

Regardless whether forward or back
Will blow the bomb – and bang all is gone

~~~

We dwell in visions of the past
          just glory – nothing will last
Always in hurry – going somewhere
Always despising what was and is
Always granting just on last wish
          which is then served on a dish
          dirty and cracked
We just lack any kind of imagination
          of presence for all the fence builders
          raising ever higher walls
          with reasons that don't call
          anything to anyone

~~~

When abstract thought cannot be put in words
When pictures in your mind for real you will never find
When the tune played by Seraphim will stay merely a dream
Call yourself blessed – but cursed even more
For the splendour you feel
Can never be shared with one other soul

~~~

When all my thoughts are blown away
And every effort to regain them fails
I try to slumber in my wake
Yet even that proves just as impossible

Frustration creeps up thus not knowing
What to do and rest just won't come

~~~

When all that's gone is lost
    And all of them that wandered still
Through darkness – fade
No light no hope
When they even stop the fight
When just everything is still
    Like non-existent – for merely a glimpse
Wondrous magical things find
    Their way into our world
And though unnoticed and not remembered – ever
    They're there and always were

~~~

When tears are shed
    And you have wept for hours without end
When secrets that been kept
    So very long now
    Are flowing on that salty river towards light
When all that what would have been bearable once
    Just becomes a martyrdom in hell
    All this swell motion blow empty

~~~

When weakness is strength and nothingness power
When crippled fools at length raise the highest tower
When odd becomes normal and manners informal
When everything that is and stands in this world

Is turned upside down – literally
It might just be the end of the beginning has come

~~~

Whether light or not
Darkness or soft
Intrigued or bored
Light-headed or just sore
Dumped into mud – spat
Filthy and cramped
All your insides yanked
      Out of their places
And when the mindless person
      You were would flee
      From horror and pain
      You now remain

~~~

Wilful ignorance stirs anger hatred
Bends and ethical perception
All is gone but yourself
And in endless oceans of sorrow
      And semiconscious aggression
Bloodlust and thirst are barely distinguishable
From thoughtful gestures of kindness and grace

~~~

2006

A race of Gods came to this world
And touched the souls of men
And left behind religion new and harsh
And no tolerance for anything else in mind
And made rules and legacies of great men
And rules then were so many that in the end
The intolerance fought over nothing

~~~

A simple harmless thought was
What brought the unspeakable into this world
And even though we fought hard
Never allowing doubts and fears
To get more than a glimpse of air
Hope crumbled and all our needs would not
Be reason enough any longer
They blamed it on that first thought
Us losing the war
And it was persecuted for good moral
What could we do
Orders are to be followed
Enemies wisdom ignored
Their lies hated and overcome
And that one simple thought destroyed
To have their foothold undone

~~~

Boredom shoots through all your veins
And all those morons sit around
Discussing words written alone so long ago
That meaning is lost and has to be found
By whoever's reading ever anew
And if for some reason you actually assume
Right from wrong, rules and faux-pas
Holy shit poetry is fucking art

~~~

Demonic dreams Massacres of old Broken hearts and
Lives 'ave been sold although unaware of reality
Hardly known facts grow elaborate cover stories
            For conspiracy theories
Whatever you do don't waver stagger or whimper
Stamping through gaping emptiness blindly
Ignoring everything and anyone that might or might
            Not be important
Judgement is complicated though always called for
            And never halted or obtained
I will not go straight into that lion's den
Not harvest the fruits of their destruction
Do have only so much time
Which is running ever faster ever fewer
Never more want more need more

~~~

Do not mean to interrupt
However that big dark nothingness
Outside does frighten me a little
Never been particularly good dealing
With that specific sort of unease
And even though your confidence
Does radiate an intense amount of strength
I might just feel better
Leaving this place to fulfil my ideas

~~~

Don't think don't doubt
Don't bother never cloud your conscience
　　　With anything anyone's problems
Never stop caring
No brief moments of regret
Always staying on that straight forward road
A highway towards your end
When however gas seems scarce
　　　Gotta lose some weight
And when passengers rebel lose them too
　　　Or tighten the belts so very much
　　　That shortly before reaching your destination
　　　You're stuck all alone and empty handed
　　　　　In the middle of nowhere
Because just wasn't good enough

~~~

Grasping the concept of a new idea
Means understanding a whole new world – in its own
Then give it a name, some time
        And once it has grown
That whole new world – of your own
        Becomes refuge
Shaping reality just as real as the common idea

~~~

Grown men fight wars 'gainst entire worlds
And all worth of mankind won't be found
        Anywhere near
If however the new kind wouldn't mind
Stepping forth ignore the old and swear their oaths
Today might be the first new age of old

~~~

Known accomplices go hunting for prey
On playgrounds in woods
Went down hand in hand
Down to the sea to cover their tracks
And whatever comes next
Nothing will sweat them nothing breaks in
And when then some time has passed by
Our friends of that night go out again
Hunting and preying and doing their deed
And after some time
Solely memories they keep

~~~

Lonely souls go wandering about
And never find no ground
Stricken hearts don't waver in their path
And still are not about
And though emotions hardly do
      Their duty these days
They rule our lives in gruesome ways
Never leaving the gutter with doubt

<div align="center">~~~</div>

Meaningful relations of empty souls
Grow never hollow
Starve though everything they hold
And even if all that has come true
      Will not be again
Me and my own won't follow the path
Suggested then

<div align="center">~~~</div>

Mind and soul of those before and
Hopes of greatness neatly stacked upon
      A pile of graceful thoughts
Met with oughts and needs taken out
And fed the hunger rough desire
Of all those bathing in Origin (a.k.a. fire)

<div align="center">~~~</div>

So I went down that predestined road
Nice and easy following most the street signs
Waiting properly in every line
Never leaving much of an impression
On anyone that happened to be travelling by
They say the way is the goal
No happy place at the end of the road
Whenever though I steer for company
Somewhere along the lane
I get ignored or they run away
Sure enough no one volunteers coming by
And those few knuckleheads trying to keep up
Too often just want me to carry their slack
And paranoia steadily catches up

~~~

The undying lands from where we came
Now shift through patterns of time
Still kings and queens in their realm
          Nut here just benign
No magic fills this world – as did the old
Just science and what we're told
The burdens to bear seem always less
When one day we manage that step
          Into our past
Let's hope without regret

~~~

When thoughts go rumbling in and out
What's real or might not be in doubt
Sun's shining disturbed by not a single cloud
Loneliness rules within this huge crowd
Nobody shares truth anymore aloud
Battling one's self makes seriously proud
And even though all thoughts hopes and dreams
Scream in your head begging to be let out
Hiding them is safer for
        The cowards we are
        The courage we don't possess
Judging thoughts we couldn't care less

~~~

2007

Bound images hold hardly anything in line
Damaged goods leave little trace within this world
Give 'em bread and water
Keep 'em fed and happy
And all the gods of men shall rise
To fight in honor of her majesty
And in likenesses of power
Grows a civilisation unheard of in future realms
So that those few fairy-tales left
Keep fluttering in and out of heads of men

~~~

Can't abide by your rule
Can't rely on not being a fool
Can't ever see beyond my little pond
And even though every bit of me
Wants so desperately a part in this world
A place to be
The unsteady stalkings of everyone else
The same doubts by them all felt
Do make it all so very hard

~~~

Can't wait to crawl out of this hole
Ever since they came and took it all away
Me myself and my brain
Won't confess to any realities of life
So that whenever it gets rough
And I might have done better
Being somewhere far away
Denial of the facts and blind stubbornness
Go on a rampage through
Whatever dares crossing my path

~~~

Dawning expectations drown in mutual disagreements
And do not follow any given rules
So all their hopes feel empty
And the hollowing suspicions of doubt
And helplessness burrow ever deeper into an abyss

~~~

Dead-beat husband will bring nothing but trouble
And though relationships often burst from inner struggle
Breaking through the boundaries of all restrictions
Can hardly count as healthy behaviour
So that in the end everybody goes back to trotting
Down their own roads, hoping desperately
To avoid one another for all time

~~~

Don't do that don't feel that
Don't go there come here
All mine not yours
Nothing's fine neither are you
Obey your orders follow all rules
Never forget that you are just you

~~~

Drama and theater in every aspect of reality
Games and manipulation so you never are free
Always guilt and evil all around
Still can't ever be without anyone
And yet how can you need other people
So desperately
That when without them on your own
You break down – go nuts
And when your loves ones do try in vain
To hold on protect and just be there
They get insulted and hurt
And can never hear the end
Of your constant complaint of their wrongdoings

~~~

Grow a pair of balls?
Dare not challenge my authority ever again
How can you have the audacity having
Your own opinion on anything
Your life is mine
Your worth is mine
And anything you ever do
Will be in reverence to me and my name

~~~

Folks that will not use their common sense
Have all those messianic hopes to maybe escape fate
And is it not moronic and utterly dense
Seeking miracles after the fact and always too late

And yet you cannot ever really expect
A life without hardship brought on by anyone's neglect
A life where the worst eventuality might just be
Nature as it once upon a time roamed free

It does sound like purest perfection too tall
Life for living flawless divine absolutely no crime
No concepts for monsters in the darkness of time
No good or bad either no distinctions at all

In the end this idea again's not thought through
Even though the dullness of that oh so safe place
Might be attractive to more than some few
This universe's mighty big – What if another race

What if without your concepts for good or bad
Without any idea of murder and mayhem of your own
Those other guys hold a gun to your head – just sad
You can't even fight back on hopes and ideas alone

~~~

Grown up voices have never travelled into
These regions and all that laughter
Would not leave
All new arrivals would not only marvel
The wonders and barely believe the
Miracles of grandeur but on top
Of all of mankind's dreams no
Nightmares evil plots or even
Conspiracy schemes

~~~

Hand out the answers
        To the meaning of life stuff
And when the forty-two points
Come to be realized
What might the ultimate question be
For meaning and origin and fate
        Are all good
And since God apologized already
        For the inconvenience
What could be bigger than that

~~~

Hatred grows
        Anger stirs all darkness in your soul won't go
I feel so left alone
        And nothing I do could ever be good enough for them
So when as a result nothing happens at all
        Just to avoid the disappointment
                Of having tried and failed

~~~

Having so little to say these days
Yet expecting way too much meaning
From all those tiny fibs of imagination
There is no wisdom in any of our faults
Wishing fate into your life might give hope
However accepting everything
And never making your own future
Will bring what little is left of
Ancient glories down to rubble

~~~

Heal my wounds and carry that
Unconscious shell into save gardens
Guard mine life and keep mine soul
That welfare of my eternal self is
             Most important
And that must surely be the hunter's goal
Me as their prey, a trophy to hunt and kill
And put upon some shelf, an adventure
             To be had
Kept and made quite unique
After all my priceless soul so rare so very
Precious must not ever return

~~~

High towers rise beyond the skies
People then fall into even deeper pits of darkness
When then they crawl out from under the earths
And see their creations in rubble
Some falter and fade

While others raise themselves
And raise new towers so much higher
Than anything that came before
So that the closed circles in which we travel
Are ever unique and ever the same

~~~

Hindsight will not brighten up
The harsh realities of life
In all the hopeful dreams
That form a thousand worlds
The grasshoppers of faith get trapped
And hardly anything works
When after all reality of here
Lets all the other worlds collapse
The of fear loneliness will never subside

~~~

Last known address last dialed glyphs
Latest fashion lonely myths
Empty words and empty planets
Eloping thought-process of dawn
Intriguing riddles irksome brightnesses
And nothing real to keep your own
With longing faithful desires
Eternity goes rumbling out
As though all pain all anger
Full of suffering could be neglected
And throughout just little time
We might eventually shine

~~~

Literary theories growing up on trees
And being picked by whoever
Might happen to stumble into
That yard of cultural studies
Of that art people do with their
Tongue on one and then put
Down on paper too

~~~

Little else dares entering that head
But hardy flaws and that intent
To one day do unlike establishment
Of character and livelihood
Though dreams rise higher always
More fears of reality are ever there
And since all men all everywhere
Do thrive on conflict more as of late
Sowing more and more hatred abroad
While neglecting home entirely
No center no own importance
No identity for myself
And neither faith nor hope can be found

~~~

Make belief lives left nothing behind
But these dead bodies down in the morgue
And even though the coroner's report
Indicates little to nothing at all helpful
To our investigations progress
Since all leads have been cold

For twenty and forty and sixty years
And so few people caring or even remembering
The traitor, the loony and the mass murderer
Will just have to go without closure

~~~

Marking the anniversary of anything and everything
And even though nothing can hold all those events
Current and commemorated we still try
And while festivities feast on heroic moments
Ceremonies and masses are gathered
For the horrific memories of death and loss
And the simple necessity of finality

~~~

More detail and so much more information to remember
Phrases in verses and killed aggression
And miracles of many minds that fade
And yet are in their broken uniqueness so much
More fascinating than anything we normneurotic
Freaks could would should ever experience
System and organisation facts with rules
On top of it all most often no personal goal
No hatred or fear. No love either?

~~~

No given thing nothing ever made easy
Everything harsh and so much evil
And though my empty dull thinking process
Does seem to produce something
My ability to do several tasks at one time
Has been severely compromised
By the dramatic lack of sleep
And those highly unusual experiences
Keep coming and there's so little
One can do to even influence
Your personal situation minimally

~~~

Seared faces little children sleeping eyes and all the victims
Of whatever brought them and us them and me into these
Dark and terrifying places
And after drowning all feelings left without emotion
Staggering throughout harsh dark deserts
When after all those centuries of death and pain and
Accepting gruesome murder as everyday life and yet
Never having seen a real corpse at least not that you
Remember and all those many bullets blast holes into
Your friends and comrades can't everything for once
Just this once turn out to be all good

~~~

That long forgotten dream of perfect worlds
In balance just and oh so true
Floats gently forward into consciousness again
And perfection is one mighty desire
We all dream our very own version of it

The blueprint is always the memory of old
Nobody considers for a second even that in truth
Present and future no matter how cruel
Are God's perfect eternal design
Balanced just certainly and very real
A sad fact only that
Light shines spotwise in an endless dark sea
Our responsibility thus is
Lighting new candles and keeping them live

~~~

The almighty nightingale sings sorrows away
Lulls minds into fretful slumber
In this omnipotence
        Of peace and chaos
The eternal balance evens out
        Dangerously strong notions
So that after all dominance wars
The dance of light goes back
        To its common shadows

~~~

The indefinable pressure on the top of your head
Dulls the mind when then you try desperately
Once in a while to keep up with discussions of culture so fine
It just won't work – everything lame
They speak of matters important and great
And you keep playing your game
And since wont just won't do – nothing there for you

~~~

When all Angels will one day come
           Down from the heavens
To bring God's Kingdom of Heaven
           To us worthless critters
The weakly humans will have to decide
Whether to give one last stand
           For their fallible nature
Or give in to some power that
So suddenly demands unquestioning
           Faith and obedience

~~~

When Christ was born
           and one god came to be the fashion of the time
When all the mayhem caused by rivalling deities
           grew into fights of men
Fights of law and land and always there and then
           how to praise God right for He in his Might
           demands worship – unquestioned faith
And those few men that used their brain
           and hungered for the same to all mankind
Heretics are and when found out
           more punishable than false worshippers

~~~

Wincing through the livelihood of men
Doing anything and everything at all times
And whenever you or I should find ourselves
In need of so many fine and necessary deeds
As can only be offered by
       Admiralty or even royalty
We can only hope beyond chance
That maybe just maybe
       All will be well

~~~

Your very personal circle of hell
Does bring consciousness to the bottom
When then flames and pain
Are absolutes of your existence
And concepts such as hope happiness content
Have become so incomprehensible
After all it does not surprise
For whenever you're about to be fleeing
The flaming circle of choice
That someone who ought to protect you love
Unconditionally
Throws you right back into the pit

~~~

2008

Angelic dreams manic hopes and feline schemes
So gracefully they stalk through flowering fields of drafting bark
In return ghosts from long ago will start their march
Towards all beauty all that lasts
The graces meet then shapes of death
Both hopelessly entangled in their dance of longing
Whatever else brought change just fades from sight
And we at war on undecided sides charge aimlessly at either
And sometimes maybe rarely ever meet some thing that follows
neither

~~~

Awe demanding struggles were decided
        In that glorious moment of fate
And we but fell into the heavens
No good way to talk yourself out of today's death
Here and now is the greatest new future
History may bring back the usual quarrels
Yet rock and trees and stories will grow
        Into shapes of life
And we immortal souls will but watch
And we daring soldiers will but be remembered

~~~

Come with me to my perfect world
I made it make it work
I rule absolute and all is well
They know the need to never care themselves
And happiness grants futures to so many more
Than this world ever dares into a generation

~~~

Deep dark secrets from sp many years ago
Long before the Age of Man
When God still walked this earth
And all the races of this world were One
And evil was not yet a word
The shadows of the future yet to come
Hung lingering and hungry all about
The First Ones all too true could not see them
Others did pick them up though
And so the dreadful fate
Would creep up always closer

~~~

Downright outrageous accusations come fluttering in
        from all corners of the galaxy
And all are in the same manner blaming us
        for the necessity of evil
While the concept's need is rather apparent
        to any sentient life form on the big scale
Being confronted with the consequences first hand
        does in so many ways spoil good moods

~~~

Drawbacks in living your life
You take it all
Worth the fight
Fuck the hell y'all
Finally overcome all my tiresome sufferings
And now it's all back
Because you just couldn't accept
Not being the center of the universe

~~~

Forgetful and slightly fretting what may or may not come
That little rather round and rather shabby man
Hushed around the corners of that way too glum city
The paranoia of watching eyes and ghastly minds following his moves
Was crushing in so harsh and whatever treasures he sought safety for
They could not possibly have weighed down more
Whatever route his lightheaded soul would take
Safety could not possibly be farther away
And in the end arrived and breathless remembering back
Forgot the papers: Shit

~~~

Freezing cold and endless empty spaces
Black and broad with tiny traces of light and life
And warmth and all that important stuff
Significance is always stuck and just so far apart
With constant yearning for the others heart

~~~

Harsh new worlds in which we go exploring
Unleash so many terrors on our homes
And geniuses in droves can hardly keep all evil out
And we go always deeper always faster
To find whatever might just possibly be found
And all this disregard of conscience
Must bring some lasting consequence
For if the current rate continues
It's just the nature of mankind
To one day out of anger or even curiosity

~~~

It came upon a midnight clear
The light and hope to shine through ages
And kings and angels rode towards it
With all of God's good graces thereof to be excused
For hope that would grant its shine
On all ravaging dudes if only they confessed
The gates of heaven can't be closed
Their victims though just can't be blessed
And will have to go - away

~~~

Know my letters learned my numbers
And still can't count my losses
Wanted so desperately to do right
Finally get my bearings – have a life
And now am stuck here
        Neither child nor made
I'd just tried to go the way expected
        Suggested and laid out straight before me

Can't figure out why it won't work
I mean I certainly do have the usual dreams of grandeur
But seriously for me want only mediocre security

~~~

Low key and fierce
Strongly marching towards eternity
Time can't fight back and
Is so very secretive by nature
Life pops up craning necks
Euphoria – a little god complex
Then suddenly so little later
Gone vanished and
Too often not even remembered

~~~

Mark up mock up lock up tight
     Contracts promises and facts of life
Fights and battles mere delight
     Always struggle always strife
More is better never pause
Can't have boring simple lives
     Can't have happiness without the fight
Always ruling someone else
     Can't ever be the lowest self

~~~

Mine my own just me
And never more and God help ye
For all punishment and crime are purely solely thine
I am great and proud and powerful
And right
And all your wailing scratching gnawing
Won't break my might
I am master know my game
I am so …
The only one still sane
And proper and right
I am in charge
And your mind can't even begin to understand
         the complexities of life I fight every day
I am while you lot only sway in motion with this world

~~~

Never ever me
Moral high ground walks easily
In those thoroughly overcrowded cells
Evil bad and so much worse
And then those subjects are of such neglect
That our grand and gracious help
Will just not be accepted
Those rotten creatures with that many
Malicious thoughts and desires
Spreading among our precious creed

~~~

No way out and still you won
Always there and yet they drowned
All visions of the future will not hold
And even though a past so bold
Brought such magnificent a manifest
Stampedes come through with much neglect

~~~

Nothing quite like the welcome sense of superiority
You walk the streets and feel the beat
You're not just a molecule in that endless swirling ocean
With certainty comes strength and much more anger
Stupid grunts can't even handle simplest tasks
And I… mean you only asked for little things to go your way
What's good for you is after all much better still for them
And in the end when enlightenment will just not come
Gotta take the spurs and make them see the way

~~~

Religion Faith and then the inevitable Apocalypse
You work your ass of
        Pray obediently
And just because that moron purposely
        Put flaws into design
Most of us can only find damnation without end
When finally his Might decides: It's Time

~~~

The might of empires new and old fades
And glows in hindsight only
Unfortunately remembering comes hard
All knowledge can these days be found
By fingertips and yet to interpret all right
Is where the challenge lies

~~~

Those fairy-tales from once upon a time
Grant morals and give precise instructions on what to do
Leave little room for life and what not
      Everything right and what not
Never you just what to do when princes ogres dragons and the
like -come knocking on your door
You need to know that doing right
Will lead to happy ever after
Even though for one - the boredom of such dullness well...
And for two - life sucks and won't let happiness last

~~~

When once upon a longing dream
You brought yourself up from under the sea of darkness
Light started shimmering through fading clouds
Finally the last few inches to the surface disappeared
Then breaking through that breath of air – a freedom hence
unknown
With limits certainly yet fully out of bounds
A world new entirely – found to be explored
And most importantly find some ground fast

~~~